# Second Helpings

## – JOY RICE –

Printed and bound in England by www.printondemand-worldwide.com

http://www.fast-print.net/bookshop

SECOND HELPINGS
Copyright © Joy Rice 2015

ISBN 978-178456-380-6

First published 2015 by
FASTPRINT PUBLISHING
Peterborough, England.

Second helpings
by Joy Rice


Dedicated to my many good friends and supporters for encouraging me to write another book. It's all your fault!


## 1 The cover explained!

For second helpings of Ecstatic Pudding,
here's the thing to do,
get all of the things that signify me,
and stick them all in some trifle or tiramisu!

Central to this concoction...
...well it's got to be Harrison Ford!
Place this legend next to a ukulele,
and decorate with a musical chord.

What else? Perhaps some strawberries?
Maybe a cat standing on some sloe gin?
How about a Bull and a Well for Bulwell?
And a porpoise skull? Might as well stick it all in!

Add a picture of Bulwell United Reformed Church,
because that's an important place to me.
Sunday services, Messy Church etcetera... I'm always there!
And...I'm often in the kitchen mashing the tea!

Better include Southwold and the lighthouse,
lots of happy memories there!
But...no matter how hard I look,
I cannot find the pier!

To balance the cover stick on a mermaid,
now, that really would be very nice.
Hang on! Look a bit closer...
...that mermaid is...Joy Rice!

Add some boiled eggs and soldiers,
as this was the illustrator's favourite childhood meal.
Beards on coat hangers? Sylvanian families?
Star wars figures? This design is quite surreal.

I needed a design for my new book cover,
and I really thought that I oughta,
ask someone who knew me well.
So, I went and asked my daughter.

Second helpings is the title of this book,
full of concoctions of my poetry.
Now, in glorious technicolour, here it is...
...a montage of images that signify me!

Thank you for my cover design.
It's unusual and really quite clever.
A fusion of poems, my life and yours,
ta very much our Heather!

*Thanks to my talented daughter Heather Morgana Rice,
illustrator, for designing the cover.*

*See more of her work on instagram.com - hevamorganarice*

# Contents

## Feelings

## Life or death?

## Men

| | |
|---|---|
| 56 | Bedroom satisfaction |
| 57 | My poem is too rude for the chip shop |
| 58 | I thought you were immortal |
| 59 | I'd like to be wined and dined... |
| 60 | If Robin Hood visited Nottingham today... |
| 61 | Richard of York Gained Battles in Vain |
| 62 | Robin Hood's bones found! |
| 63 | Robin Williams |
| 64 | Scotsmen |
| 65 | Snoring |
| 66 | Switch your mobile on |
| 67 | We've never had to consult a solicitor yet |
| 68 | Yul Brynner kind of way |

## Oddities

| | |
|---|---|
| 69 | Camera phone |
| 70 | Freddie is a good boy |
| 71 | My cat, Missy |
| 72 | That's where the sea comes in |
| 73 | The war will be over by Christmas |
| 74 | Waterworks |
| 75 | We're not in the same wavelength |
| 76 | You'll never be in my quiz team |

## Religious stuff

| | |
|---|---|
| 77 | God loves me |
| 78 | Green church cups |
| 79 | If Heaven has a flavour it must be coffee |
| 80 | Lord's Prayer banned |
| 81 | Palm Sunday Donkey |
| 82 | Saint |
| 83 | Some people say Christians are cracked! |

Please note – numbers refer to the poems and not the pages.

**Bulwell**   - poems about the place where I live.


2   Aldi in Bulwell


When we heard the news in Bulwell Village,
everyone shouted hooray!
Aldi was opening a store on Bulwell Forest,
to be open before Christmas Day!

But...Christmas day came and went,
and no sign of our new Aldi store.
So we had to shop at Tesco's,
just like we'd done before.

Every time we walked passed the site;
we wondered what was the score?
Why the delay? Why is no work going on?
When would we get our local Aldi store?

Questions were asked to our councillors,
but no-one seemed to know...
...rumours abounded...like wildflowers on Bulwell Forest,
 it seemed like Aldi was on a go slow!

Someone said there was a petrol tank,
that had been left by the former garage,
and there were whispers and mutterings of
shenanigans and somebody said "sabotage"!

But...then we heard the real news,
and we all sighed with dismay!
There's a one hundred metre well under the site,
and that's what is causing the delay!


One hundred metres down! Oh my! That's terribly deep!
In fact it's flipping whopping!
So until they sort that out,
we'll have to make alternative plans for our shopping.


We can't wait to have Aldi within walking distance,
but...you know that it is full well.
Aldi should have realised...the clue is in the name...
That there's a massive well in Bulwell!


*At the time of publishing...*

*....we are still awaiting our new Aldi store!*

*But...there are rumours of Lidl coming to Bulwell!*

## 3    Ay up! Them boggers!

Ay up! Them boggers!
Trying to impress their swanky mates,
by using East Midlands expressions.
Ay up me duck! Int it great!


You could've knocked me dahn wiv a fevver,
its gospel truth, by all that's holy!
For at the Hollywood Film Awards,
who should say it but - Angelina Jolie!


And now - guess what?
It's all the craze! It's going global.
Prince Harry's saying "Ay up me duck!"
Makes it kind of noble!


I wonder who'll say it next?
The whole thing could go amuck!
Let's take the world by storm!
Come on - Ay up me duck!


*Written after reading in the paper – "Actress Angelina Jolie left some
audience members baffled when she greeted Derby actor Jack
O'Connell with "ay up me duck" at an awards ceremony. She spoke in
a Derby accent and introduced him with the East Midlands phrase as
she presented him with an award at the Hollywood Film Awards".*

## 4    Badly in Bulwell

It's black ovver Bill's muvvers. There's summat up wi me.
Ah'm all of a puther, berra mash a pot a tea.

I feel like I've lost a tanner,
I'm norrayin no tuffees!
I think I've gorra code cummin,
gorra nankey in case I'll sneeze.

Ah'm feeling proper badly. Mi duck, I dunt feel alrate.
Ey up, don't call mi mardy. Am gerrin in a state.

There's nowt I can do abaht it.
Feeling proper off, ah yoof,
I'm really feelin dead pawleh,
Mi duck, int  that the troof.

Think I'll go for a walk on the causey.
Gerroff down to Bulwell Bogs orl by missen,
tek mi snap or gerra sucker,
mekkin mi rate as ninepence agen.

Bulwell Bogs can lift ya spirits,
allus summat gud to see.
Ducks swimmin on the watter,
Bulwell's alrate bi mi.

*I've been experimenting with local dialect!*
*Well, if it's good enough for Angelina...*
*Also - Thanks to Paul Turton (photographer extraordinaire and*
*author of the Bulwell then and Now books) who added my*
*voice to his picture of Bulwell Bogs and posted on YouTube -*
*https://www.youtube.com/watch?v=PiSKIAcvNYk*

## 5   Bulwell Bogs - what a great place to be!


Bulwell Bogs - what a great place to be!
In the summer it's like being at Bulwell on sea.


Our children can paddle in the River Leen.
It's got a green flag award for being so clean!


There's a water park to play in and have lots of fun.
A perfect place to spend a day out, in the sun.


There's ducks on the river and fishes there too!
Depending on which way you are looking...
                                    ... there's a great view!


There's flower beds planted with perennial flowers.
You can walk along the river to while away the hours.


There's cherry trees planted with free fruit for the picking.
And there's bound to be an ice cream van with ices for licking.


If Bulwell Bogs was anywhere else you'd think what a delight!
And do you know what? You would be quite right!

But, because it's in Bulwell and called The Bogs.
It summons up visions of mucky locals in clogs.
It creates an image of dirty old dogs,
and a river full of refuse, rubbish and frogs.


But if Bulwell was Stratford,
 on the River Avon's banks.
You'd say well done to Bulwell,
 and give heartfelt thanks,
to the people who campaigned and fought,
 to keep it for the community.
We now have a great water and play park,
 (hopefully) for posterity!


So, let's celebrate Bulwell,
with cheers and elation,
and if you want to use the bogs in Bulwell...
                    ...well they are near the bus station.

## 6  Bulwell is a great place!

Bulwell is a great place!
Let's all keep it clean!
Don't drop your litter in the street.
Don't chuck it in the Leen.

If your doggie does a whoopsie
Please, please be a fast mover.
Pick it and dispose of it properly,
don't leave it for the Council's Poover.

If you're having a takeaway.
don't leave your litter for others to clear up.
Please take away your wrappers and bags.
Please take away any can, bottle or cup.

Let's all work together.
Stop being messy – come on let's quit.
It doesn't take much effort.
We all just need to do our bit.

Let's have some pride in Bulwell.
It's really a great place to be.
and it would be so much nicer,
 if the streets were all litter- free.

Bulwell is a great place!
Celebrate with me!
Let's all be proud of Bulwell!
And keep Bulwell litter-free!

*This was written in response to a request from Celia Knight –*
*Bulwell Neighbourhood Development Officer.*

## 7  Crocodiles in the Leen

I've just heard something shocking,
about something that I've never seen.
But... did you know that in Bulwell,
there are crocodiles in the River Leen?


I guess it must be because the water,
is pure and fresh and clean.
The perfect environment and habitat,
for those crocodiles in the River Leen.


I know that from now onwards,
that I'm really not too keen,
and I don't think I'll be paddling,
with those crocodiles in the River Leen.


I hope those crocs are friendly.
I hope they're not being mean.
I hope they don't pinch the bread from the ducks,
those crocodiles in the River Leen.


*Henry Stapleton wondered if there are crocodiles in the River Leen – so I wrote a poem about it!*

## 8  First day of Spring in Bulwell

It's the first day of spring in Bulwell,
and it seems like it has been for a while.
I went for a long walk along Piccadilly,
seeing the cherry blossom made me smile.


I wandered along Highbury Vale,
admiring Poppy's display of Daffs all lovely and yellow.
Then I stopped at the Co-op,
and chattered with an old Bulwell fellow.


I moseyed on down through Deptford Crescent,
thought I'd have a walk along the River Leen.
Lots of Spring - nature in abundance,
and fishes - cos the river is clean.


I strolled among the stalls on the market,
and then walked along the Main Street.
It's marvellous when you're out in Bulwell,
you never know who you might meet.

The Spring sunshine brings everyone out.
Everyone is friendly and full of pep.
Let's hope that this sunshine stays with us,
cos it's put a real Spring in our step!

## Frosty day in Bulwell

It's a sunny day in Bulwell!
But, it's freezing cold out there.
Although the sun is shining,
the frost is sparkling everywhere.


It's really very nippy,
and everything is covered in rime.
It would inspire me to write a poem,
if only I could find a rhyme?


It's a glorious day in Bulwell!
The frost is sparkling in the sun.
Don't be put off by the cold.
Put your thermals on, get out and have some fun!


One good thing about the frost,
is that it kills off all the bugs and germs.
So, you might as well enjoy the frost,
until the warm weather returns!

Me Mam smacked the Bulwell out of me.
She sed, "Speak the Queen's English just like me.
Our kid you'll come a cropper,
if you don't learn to talk proper".
Oh me Mam smacked the Bulwell out of me.

If I sed I was off to muck abawt on t'causey.
Me Mam'd cause a fuss and chastise me.
She sed, "Ow menny times av you bin towd,
not to play out on the bleddy road!"
Oh me Mam smacked the Bulwell out me.

Sometimes I would get up to fun and mischief,
me Mam'd have a fit and cause me grief.
She sed, "Watch it clever clogs.
and gerroff dahn to Bulwell Boggs".
Oh me Mam smacked the Bulwell out me.

No matter how hard I tried I cudn't talk posh
I'd say "flippin eck" ... never golly or gosh.
Dropped haitches from mi words caused howls!
And I mangled up mi vowels.
Oh me Mam smacked the Bulwell out me.

Oh me Mam smacked the Bulwell out me.
Guess I never can speak English properly.
You know that it is full well,
you can take this girl out of Bulwell,
but, you can't smack the Bulwell out of me!

*Another attempt at dialect and set to music as a song that I
perform (on the ukulele) as part of my Poetry Performances.*

## 11    There's a shortage of ducks in Bulwell!

There's a shortage of ducks in Bulwell!
Not real ones, but those of the plastic kind,
you can search all the charity shops...and the market,
but, not one plastic duck will you ever find!


There's a shortage of ducks in Bulwell!
No sign of a 'paddling of ducks' on the River Leen.
No plastic, ceramic or wooden ones...
...no toy ducks anywhere to be seen!


There's a shortage of ducks in Bulwell!
Not even a duckling anywhere on sale.
I've heard that they've all been taken,
to that new Bulwell Farm on Highbury Vale.


There's a shortage of ducks in Bulwell!
Of ducks we are out of luck!
But, if you go to Bulwell Farm early in the morning,
you might just see one and say, "Ey up miduk!"


*Inspired by my friend, Charles Towlson, who created the*
*whimsical Bulwell Farm and won an award from*
*Nottingham in Bloom!*

## 12    William Peverel

Listen up my friends to this tale I have to tell,
about a Norman knight called William Peverel.

He came to England with William the Conqueror,
it's rumoured that Bill was his dad.
They fought at the battle of Hastings.
They won. We lost. Too bad!

For his support in battle, he was rewarded,
William the conqueror honoured him full well,
He gave him one hundred manors in Central England,
and the best of those manors was in Bulwell!

By the time 1086 came along,
his manors numbered one hundred and sixty two,
Nottingham Castle, Peverel Castle in Castletown,
Derbyshire,
just to name a few!

Back in the day, William was popular.
I guess you could say renown.
To tell you the truth, I'd never heard of him!
I only knew Peverel Street in town.

Now, if you want to learn about William Peverel,
Google him, go on Wikipedia and have a look!
Or if you can get a hold of an old copy...
...well, you'll find a mention of him in the Domesday Book.

Now, William's name is remembered in Bulwell.
right in Bulwell's main hub.
For J.D Wetherspoons have immortalised him,
by putting his name on their pub!


So, let's all remember William Peverel,
come on, charge up your beers!
Let's drink a toast to William Peverel.
Everybody say cheers!


*Written and performed for the Bulwell Arts Festival 2015
and 2016.*

*For more information about The Bulwell Arts Festival
https://bulwellartsfestival.com/*

# Christmas and other special days!

*A selection of poems for various occasions!*

## 13   Christmas ads

There's Christmas ads on TV,
that tug at your heart strings.
Lots of images of family fun,
and all sorts of wonderful things!

There's Christmas lights up in the town,
trees and decorations everywhere.
But where is there a nativity scene?
I can't see one anywhere.

There's plenty of Christmas spirit about,
wine, liquor and plenty of booze.
Buy one get one free offers.
Tell me, how can you refuse?

There's queues in the supermarket,
people buying food for a feast.
But what about all those without?
Can we share a little....at least?

Where is the true spirit of Christmas?
The reason that we all celebrate.
We're supposed to remember a special baby,
not to pile up the food on our plate!

Remember the food banks this Christmas.
Remember the poor and the lost.
Remember Christ born in poverty.
Remember to give without counting the cost.


Share what you have this Christmas.
Let's see what good you can achieve.
Christmas is a time for sharing and giving,
and it's better to give than to receive!


*For more information about our local foodbank*
*http://bestwoodbulwell.foodbank.org.uk/*

## 14    Christmas without you

We're getting ready for Christmas.
There's so much work to do.
We're writing out our Christmas cards.
But...it won't be the same without you.

We're getting ready for Christmas.
We're full of Christmas cheer.
We're making lists and shopping.
But...it's no fun if you're not here.

We're getting ready for Christmas.
We've trimmed up our Christmas Tree.
We've chocolate, treats and goodies.
But...I'd rather have you here with me.

We're getting ready for Christmas.
We're putting on a brave face.
Life goes on ...so they say...
But...I want you...not this empty space.

We're getting ready for Christmas.
Christmas time is for family and friends.
So, we'll think of you and happy times,
memories and love never ends.

*Remembering those friends and family who can't be with us at Christmas...or any other time.*

## 15 It must be Madness!

Special Star twinkling in the sky.
Magi looking and wondering why?
Following it as it flies by.
It must be Madness!

Evil King Herod - no one can deny.
Pretenders to the throne must die!
Herod really is a bad guy.
It must be Badness!

Census - everyone must comply.
No room at the inn - oh my!
Shelter needed somewhere dry.
It must be Sadness!

Shepherds, sheep and dogs...come by!
Angels Hallelujahing on high.
Rejoicing at that baby's cry.
It must be Gladness!

Christ the baby born to die.
Saviour sent for you and I.
Wonder why?
It must be Madness!

## 16 <u>Merry Christmas from Bulwell!</u>

Merry Christmas from Bulwell!
Sending you good wishes galore.
Good health, good wealth, good times,
for this Christmas and many more!

Whatever you wish for (in reason),
I hope that it's coming your way.
May the blessings and love of Christmas,
be with you each and every day!

Enjoy this day and the next ones,
time passes by so swift.
Savour each day as it comes to you;
remember...each day is a gift!

## 17    The brussels have crosses on their bottoms.

The brussels have crosses on their bottoms.
The turkey is thawing in the sink.
I can no longer get into my pantry,
as it's all full of crisps and drink.

The potatoes have all been peeled.
The veggies are primped and prepped.
The Christmas tree is all lit up.
The halls are all Holly be-decked.

I've posted all of my Christmas cards,
and tramped around Bulwell delivering the rest!
I've spoken to so many people on my travels;
I really am so very very blest!

I've seen several Nativities. I've watched Christmas films on TV.
The Christmas CD is playing. The presents are under the tree.

The mince pie is ready for Santa.
There are carrots for the reindeers too!
It's Christmas Eve in Bulwell.
Hope that there is nothing else to do!

So, as I sit and ponder...
...all this preparation to celebrate Jesus birth...
...I pray that next year... What do you think?
Will we ever have Peace on Earth?
So, let's have Peace where we live,
whether it's Bulwell, Bangkok or Bethlehem!
Let Peace ripple out and spread everywhere,
Goodwill to all women and to all men!

## 18 Happy New Year from Bulwell!

A New Year heralds a new start.
A blank page to fill with new things.
So, make the most of this New Year,
and make the best of whatever life brings.

If opportunity comes knocking,
then be sure to open the door!
Don't let chances pass by you,
grab them and look for some more!

Don't bother with resolutions;
you know that they are hard to stick to!
Just resolve to be open to new experiences,
a New Year so maybe try something new?

Whatever this New Year brings,
I hope that it's perfect for you.
Good health, good friends, good times,
and may you succeed in all that you do!


## 19 January 10th - Peculiar People Day

According to my calendar,
January 10th is Peculiar People Day.
I had to Google it to be sure,
but it is! So what more can I say?
So, Happy Peculiar People Day,
to all friends odd and weird.
Sending you best wishes,
to show you that I've cared!

## 20   Jan 12th - Kiss a Ginger Day

Oh happy day! To celebrate those people with red hair!
A day to kiss a ginger to show just that we care!
But...can I just walk up to a ginger person and bestow on them a kiss?
Perhaps they'll think I'm wappy? They'll wonder what's amiss?

So, maybe I'll just smile instead and say a cheery Hello!
Because although kissing is nice, you can't do it to someone you don't know.
A smile is always welcome...and I don't want to be a whinger...
....but let's have a day to be nice to everyone, blonde, brunette or ginger!

## 21   March 21st - World Poetry Day

I've just had an email from Amazon,
trying to sell me a poetry book or two or three,
to celebrate World Poetry Day on March 21st.
Now...why did no one tell me?

I didn't know that poets had a special poetry day.
I'd have written a poem to celebrate.
And why are Amazon only just telling me?
Crikey they're two days late!

So...to celebrate poets, writers and authors.
My friend, Gary, tells me that it's really hard...to be a bard.
Happy World Poetry Day - two days late.
Next year I'll remember and send a card!

*With thanks to Gary Davis who suggested the rhyme*
*'it's hard to be a bard'.*

## 22 <u>May 4th- Happy International Star Wars day!</u>

Happy International Star Wars day!
May the force forever be with you!
May you always stand up for,
all that is good and true.


May your light sabre always shine brightly.
May you have the courage of a Jedi knight.
May you always stand up for,
all that you know to be right.


May you never be scared of the bad guys.
May you always have a positive view.
May you live long and prosper!
And may the force always be with you!


*For all those Star Wars fans out there – especially my grandson, Oliver, who missed being born on Star Wars Day...by just one day!*

I can see from the calendar that you made for me,
that today is Bad Poetry Day!
Is there some kind of message here for me?
Is there something that you're trying to say?


You know how I like rhyming couplets,
even if my poems don't always scan.
But, I try to write poems that I hope people like.
Honestly! I'm doing the best that I can!


I know that I'll never write like Shakespeare,
or Byron or Wordsworth or Nash.
I'll never be famous like John Cooper Clarke;
I'll never make loads of cash.


But, rhyming is always in my mind,
you could say poetry is in my DNA.
So, I'll make the most of this 'gift'???
And celebrate Bad Poetry Day!

## Experiences

24      <u>Don't judge a book by its cover.</u>

Don't judge a book by its cover.
You really should look inside.
You don't know what you'll discover.
You might be surprised and satisfied.

Don't be put off by the daft title,
or the picture of that mad woman with the umbrella.
You might find a poem that is vital.
You might get it before it's a best seller.   (In her dreams)

So, don't judge my book by its cover.
Please DO look inside!
Who knows what poems you'll uncover?
You never know till you've tried!


*Always trying to plug Ecstatic Pudding!*



25      <u>Good deeds</u>

Practice Random Acts of Kindness!
That's what our community needs!
Think how happy we all would be,
if everyone performed good deeds.

A good deed doesn't cost a penny,
but can be priceless to the person who receives it.
A good deed gives a positive feeling,
to the person who achieves it!

A good deed can be a simple thing,
without hardly any effort on your part.
But, the act of doing it and helping others,
is so warming to the heart!

We all of us need to feel useful.
We all need a purpose in life.
No one goes looking for trouble.
No one searches for strife.

Some of us seem to have everything,
no worries, no troubles and not a care.
While others struggle with life's heavy burdens,
which can be lifted if we all support and share.

Your good deed can be spontaneous,
or it could even be planned.
I bet we all know someone...?
...who would be glad of a helping hand!

So, take some time to think what you can do,
to help others in our community.
It costs nothing to be pleasant and say "Hello",
and smiles come for free!

Please practice those Random Acts of Kindness.
Let's all help each other out.
Good Deeds - free to everyone.
Let's spread some happiness about!

*Suggested by Bill Blackamore for the Evening Post Good Deeds campaign 2015 and I, subsequently, read out at our Lord Mayor's awards night when Bill received a long service volunteer award. Congratulations and Well done, Bill!*

## 26     <u>I forgot!</u>

There's something I had to do...
On the tip of my tongue and on my fingertips...
...Oh yes! I was supposed to get special glasses.
Bugger! I missed that flipping eclipse.


## 27     <u>I only went out to buy milk...</u>

I only went out to buy milk...
But I was tempted by BOGOF offers.
So, I purchased things I didn't need,
putting cash into the supermarket's coffers.

I only went out to buy milk...
But, I discovered bargains in the end of line bin.
So, I bought one or two just in case,
as far as I could see it was a win - win!

I only went out to buy milk...
But, there were cheap items just up to their sell by date.
So, I just had to buy them...of course,
I can't resist a bargain...they're great!

I only went out to buy milk...
And I came home loaded up, with ever such a lot.
I only went out to buy milk...
So guess what? ...It was milk that I forgot!

If I was President of the world,
now wouldn't that be just great?
Wars would be banned, peace would be in.
Everyone would be my mate.

If I was President of the world,
I'd want everyone to share the world's wealth.
I'd make medical care free for everyone,
so that we could all benefit from good health.

If I was President of the world,
I'd make taxation fair.
So that everyone contributes what they can,
everybody pays their share.

If I was President of the world,
I'd ban poverty (and greed?).
I'd share the world's resources,
so that everyone has just what they need.

If I was President of the world, now wouldn't that be splendid!
I'd have an open policy, absolutely nothing would be hid.

If I was President of the world,
now wouldn't that be surreal?
I'd be feeling on top of the world...
...but I wonder how everyone else would feel?

Guess...I'll never be President of the world.
To wish for it makes me a dope!
So, instead I'll wish for peace, compassion,
friendship and love and a great big dollop of hope!

## 29   Kindred spirits

There's something about you that I like.
I'm not sure what it is?
But as kindred spirits go,
you really are the biz!

We're always on the same wavelength.
We're singing from the same hymn sheet.
I think that you and I,
go together just a treat!

We have similar opinions.
We nearly always agree.
And if there ever was a fault,
well...it wouldn't be with me!

## 30   Knit and Knatter

If you want to put the world to rights,
and discuss the important things that matter.
What better place is there for a debate?
Than at your local Knit and Knatter!

If you fancy a discussion on politics,
religion, sex or this and that.
Then seek out the conversation
at the nearest Craft and Chat.

If you relish a good gossip,
on saucy topics that enrich.
My dear...there's only one place to go,
and that's at the Stitch and Bitch!

*I was challenged to write a poem about knit and natter by a*
*lady at a group that I gave a talk to.*

## 31    Overactive bladder

Well hey up...here's the latest;
I've now got to retrain my bladder!
It's working when it shouldn't do;
it's overactive...what could be sadder?

I've got to increase my fluid intake,
and teach my bladder how to hold it,
and if it forgets and let's it drop...
...then I don't have to scold it.

I'm thinking of calling my bladder Fido,
as we embark on this training regime,
of pelvic floor exercises, omitting certain foods,
no carbonated drinks and no caffeine!

Now...I can cut out the caffeine,
as I have done for years...
...but did you know it was in chocolate?
I'm now in different floods...of tears?

So me and Fido are in this together,
we're going to give it our very best.
Let's hope that this bladder calms down,
and passes the pelvic floor test.

It really isn't amusing...
...some days I feel that Fido is just like a sieve,
and let's face it - yes it's funny...
....it's the only part of me that's overactive!

We planned a trip to Anglesey!
A planned meet-up-reunion...
                    ...We planned to have a good time.
But... we hadn't planned on it raining,
 so we played cards and drank champagne and wine.


We planned to revisit old places,
we planned a beach walk in the sunshine.
But... we hadn't planned on it raining,
 so we played cards and drank champagne and wine.


We planned to have lots of nice meals...
...and I must admit that the cod and chips were divine!
But we hadn't planned on it raining,
 so we played cards and drank champagne and wine.


We planned to have a good catch-up together,
and it was good to have plenty of time.
But, we hadn't planned on it raining,
so we played cards and drank champagne and wine.


The last time we went to Anglesey,
we were camping...and the weather was fine.
But we hadn't planned on it raining...this time,
 so we played cards and drank champagne and wine.


I don't think that we had really planned it...
...but despite the rain, we all had a good time.
And much as I wanted to revisit Anglesey...
It was a long way to go to play cards and drink champagne
and wine!

We're planning another trip together in two years' time.
I'm going to check the weather forecast for signs of rain.
Although I love meeting up with my good friends,
I don't plan to be playing cards, drinking wine and
champagne!


*Thank you to my lovely friends, Evelyn Henry, José Mason
and Debbie Thornhill for planning this great trip to
Anglesey! A celebration for my 60<sup>th</sup> birthday!*

33      Shopping

I wanted a new shopping experience;
I was looking for something more intense and deeper.
I thought I'd explore the 99pence store;
disappointingly... it was the same as Poundland....
                                        ...Only cheaper!

34  Winter sunshine

            It's great to see the sunshine in the winter.
            It's lovely to feel sun-kissed.
            But...when the sun shines into my house,
            it highlights all of the dusting that I've missed.

# Feelings

## 35    Dance in the rain!

Don't let the storm clouds bother you,
they'll soon be gone away.
Enjoy today for what it is.
Celebrate today!

Make the most of what life brings,
happiness...strife... or pain...
...The storm will pass...but 'till it does...
...Lets' just dance in the rain!

*Hello Lovely!*
*One of the many poems inspired by my lovely friend,*
*Alison Hadley.*

## 36    Ex best friends

I saw you just the other day.
It caught me unawares.
I can't remember when we last met;
it must be years and years.

We used to be such perfect pals,
our friendship was so strong!
I can't remember how we broke up,
where did it all go wrong?

We used to go on holidays,
one time we even shared a bed!
What happened to end our friendship?
Was it something that I said?

We used to spend all of our time together,
going out or staying in watching TV.
We were so much in sync together;
I thought we would be friends for all eternity.

Then one day, you didn't want to play.
and then the next day too.
You'd moved on, found other friends,
you had better things to do.

I recollect that some years later,
we tried to fix what we had broken.
But, the cracks were always there,
and truths were left unspoken.

So...we move on with our busy lives.
For the past - I don't know how to make amends.
I wish you well, wish you all the best,
and remember when we were the best of friends.

*When we are children, we think that we will be friends
forever...but life happens and we grow apart.
However...I am very blessed to have some really special
friends that I have made...as an adult...and childhood
friends that I still keep in touch with.*

## 37    Green washing up bowl

There isn't much that I crave for;
I'm such a simple soul.
But, I just had to have it,
when I saw a green washing-up bowl.

I nearly chose a purple one,
now that would have been really bitchin',
but, I didn't really think that it,
would go well with my kitchen.

No, the green bowl it had to be,
and at £1.49 a bargain price!
It fits in well with my colour scheme.
I think it looks jolly nice!

Denis thought it was unnecessary,
he said, "it's just a load of plastic,
we've got one anyway, why replace?"
He couldn't see that I thought it was fantastic!

We had words in Aldi.
We nearly had a row.
He couldn't see that I wanted a new bowl...
...and I wanted it NOW!

We might have a bowl at home,
but it's getting shabby and ol',
and what's wrong with girl treating herself,
to a brand new washing up bowl?

He said I was using up the planet's resources,
and I should think of my carbon footprint.
A handy argument for him to make,
to cover up being a mean skinflint.

I DO care about our planet,
love, peace and harmony is my goal.
So, I'm sorry Mother Nature, Father Time and God,
but, I just want a new washing-up bowl!

At £1.49 it's cheaper than a pint of beer,
cheaper than wine, flowers or chocolate.
So, shut up I'm buying this washing up bowl...
...and you must admit my sink looks great!


*Dedicated to all people everywhere who crave new
washing up bowls!*

## 38 I sometimes stumble over my words

I sometimes stumble over my words.
Can't always think what to say.
I try to say one thing,
but it comes out another way.


I've been concerned that I'm getting Alzheimer's.
I'm worried that I'm losing the plot.
But, really there's a simple explanation,
for this memory thingy, wotsit that I've got.


Hold on to your hats!
Now let me thrill and amaze yer...
...For I was told by a "friend",
that what I have is called nominal aphasia!


Nominal is a fancy word for names.
Aphasia is for comprehension.
I'm hoping that what I have is normal ageing,
and no other brain stuff, I'd rather not mention!

## 39   <u>I wish I could kick ass</u>

I wish I could kick ass, seriously,
like Bruce Willis in Die Hard.
I'd kick those baddies butts,
and I'd leave my calling card.

I'd right wrongs, I'd do good,
I'd be in and out just like a ninja.
I'd sort out all the bad guys,
and I'd not care if I'd injure.

I'd be an avenging angel,
I'd give the rascals a good slap.
I'd get rid of all the villains,
I wouldn't take any crap.

I'd give them a good slap upside the head,
I wouldn't pussyfoot about.
I'd make them sorry for what they had done.
I'd make sure that they were taken out.

I'd clear up all the dross.
I'd make everything all right.
I just wish I had the muscles,
and physique to give them a real good fright!

## 40    Impatience

I know that I ought to be patient,
but, you try the patience of a saint.
Observing your inaction,
is like watching drying paint.

You faff and fanny about,
taking faffing to a whole new level.
Your prevarication is driving me nuts.
You are the very devil!

I know I ought to be patient,
but, really this is a farce.
Come on! Get your act together!
What you need is a kick up the arse!

## 41    Is there still a light at the end of the tunnel?

Is there still a light at the end of the tunnel?
Or did someone forget to turn it on?
Do bluebirds still fly over the rainbow?
Or have they all flown off and gone?

Is my glass half full or half empty?
Or did it all evaporate away?
Is it true that a cuppa cures everything?
Can tea really keep my troubles at bay?

Will it really be better tomorrow?
After I've had a good night's rest...
....or will life be still a trial,
a tribulation, trouble and a test?

They say that laughter is the best medicine;
at least it's good 'cause it's free.
But...sometimes I really do wonder...
...is it the rest of the world...or is it just me?


42      Just Desserts

When anxieties start to bloom and grow,
and worries begin budding.
Remember STRESSED is DESSERTS spelt backwards,
so, why not cure yourself with pudding?

Emotions can be troubling,
and sometimes feelings hurts.
Grab yourself some pudding!
Get your just desserts!

Feeling stressed is serious;
the symptoms can make you sick.
Really it's no laughing matter;
make an appointment for medical help, quick!

## 43 <u>Misplaced motivation</u>

I seem to have misplaced my motivation.
I thought I had it here,
but, when I went searching for it,
it had vanished into thin air!

I looked for it down the back of the settee.
No motivation could I find.
This reminds me of the time,
when I thought I'd lost my mind.

I hunted for it in the garden,
searching underneath shrubs and plants.
I found lots of interesting creatures,
but, motivation - not a chance!

I pondered and I had a thought, maybe, it's hidden in a book.
But, motivation I couldn't find, no matter how hard I'd look.

What is it with motivation? I've found to my great cost,
that when motivation is needed, it's often always lost.

I think maybe someone is telling me,
that I need to relax and chill,
because when you're not looking for it,
motivation comes - it always will.

So, maybe I need to stop overthinking,
Maybe, this is what I should learn.
Take a break, now and then - it is ok!
Because motivation will surely return.

*A Facebook friend, Jennie, had posted that she had misplaced
her motivation – result inspiration to me for a poem!*

## 44    <u>One of those days</u>

I'm having quite a time of it.
I'm having 'one of those days';
I feel that the world is conspiring against me,
in, oh, so many ways.

The telephone keeps on ringing,
but, not one of the calls is for me.
Just telephone message about PPIs,
or someone asking if I want a telephone protection policy.

I hung my washing out because it was sunny,
but, now it's started to rain.
And, I forgot to switch the oven on,
so, there is no dinner ...again!

I've lost my keys,
I've looked and looked ...but keys I cannot find.
I've lost my flipping marbles,
and I think that I must be losing my mind!

There are bills in the post instead of letters,
and junk mail and menus galore.
The best way to deal with them is to chuck them,
because that's what the recycling bin is for.

I got out of the bed on the wrong side.
Life's unravelling, I'm losing my thread.
Think I'll have a duvet day,
and just go back to bed instead!

## 45   Such sorrow when I heard the news

Such sorrow when I heard the news.
The government has consented to war.
I know that we need to get involved in military action,
and terrorism is something that we cannot ignore.

Such sorrow when I heard the news.
What is this world coming to?
When a good man is cruelly slaughtered,
for having a different point of view.

Such sorrow when I heard the news.
Tears in my eyes and heart beating fast.
When will humankind give peace a chance?
And why can't peace ever last?


*Such sorrow when I heard of the execution of Alan Henning
the ex-cabbie and volunteer humanitarian aid worker.*

## Life or death?

46      <u>Advance Decision - Living will??</u>

When Heaven calls, "your time is up!"
My! Won't that be great!
So, if you find me, passed away,
please don't resuscitate!

If I'm sat all flippy and floppy,
and bits of me start to sag.
Check my pulse; make sure I've left,
before you stuff me in a body bag.

When my time is up, when I've had my span,
then let me go, don't wait.
If my ticker has stopped ticking,
please don't defibrillate!


*We have a defibrillator at our Church – please don't use it on me – let me go!*

## 47     Death's door

I might have been at Death's door,
but, Death must have been out.
It wasn't time for me to go,
of that there is no doubt.

I'm not ready to fall off my perch.
Not ready to bite the dust.
Not ready to push up daisies.
Not ready to be flushed.

I'm not ready to shuffle off my mortal coil.
Not ready to kick the bucket.
Not ready to pop my clogs.
Not ready for death - I'll duck it!

I'm not ready to join the choir invisible.
Not ready to take the train to glory.
Not ready to go to the Promised Land.
I want to stay and finish my story.

I'm here for a little bit longer,
this is my second, third or fourth chance.
So, I'm going to make the most of life.
Sing, celebrate and dance!

*Inspired by my brother, Roy Garside, who had been ill and
said that he'd been at Death's door.*

## 48    Drink your way out of Dementia

The latest research in keeping Alzheimer's and Dementia at bay,
is to drink three glasses of champagne each and every day!

There's a compound that boosts spatial memory,
that's found in champagne.
So, drinking three glasses daily is good for the brain!

Academics at Reading University,
have been experimenting on rats,
and now they are looking for pensioners...
... to test and check out their stats.

So, where do you apply? Where do I volunteer?
I don't mind quaffing champers...it'll make a change from beer!

Do they deliver it to your house? Is this champagne for free?
I suppose I could force myself to drink it, if it's to help humanity!

So, bring on the Bollinger, Moët & Chandon and Veuve Clicquot!
I've got my pint pot here ready, come on, I'm good to go!

Now, if you see me acting doolally...
... and you suspect I'm "off my trolley",
I won't have Alzheimer's; I'll have just had too much Bolly!


*I read about this research this in the newspaper.*
*Just google – Champagne and Dementia – you'll be surprised!*

## 49    Inheritance

My Mother was a little dumpy woman.
My Father was tall and thin.
So... why did I inherit my Mother's fat genes?
Why couldn't I be tall and thin like him?

I've inherited my Dad's dodgy chest...
...You should hear me pant and wheeze.
I've also inherited Dad's hairy legs,
and I've even got his knobbly knees!

Mum's passed on her bloody blood pressure,
and it's always flippin high!
I've even got her excessive cholesterol,
can't lower it – not matter how hard I try!

I've inherited my Dad's lovely blonde hair,
and I've got the same grey eyes.
But why did I have to get my Mum's dodgy vision?
I think that must be the booby prize!

I've not got Mum's love of dusting...
...but I think I've also got her OCD.
As I'm always plumping up cushions...
..straightening pictures – it's just got to be perfect for me.

On a positive note there's some good stuff too,
it's really not all too bad.
There's my love of films, books and poetry,
that I acquired from my dear old Dad.

Mum loved to bake and have friends around for tea,
and I think I've got her amazing baking gift.
I've even got her wooden rolling pin...
..how about that for recycling and thrift?

I've got both their 'love of family',
and knack of making and keeping friends.
I've copied their example of loving and caring,
and hope that it never ends.

I'm thankful for their influence,
and all of the things that they taught me,
I know that their love and nurturing,
has shaped the person that is me!

I think that I look a bit like them...
Hey...I've got Dad's dimple in my chin.
I'm thankful for those genes they passed on...
...But I still wish I'd inherited tall and thin!


*For my Mum and Dad –*
*Lillian Margaret Garside (nee Shellam)*
*and Thomas Edward Garside.*

Life is full of adversity, with trials and troubles galore.
I sometimes wonder what it's all about? What is it all for?
Life has its ups but sometimes...too many downs.
I sometimes wonder if bad stuff is just going the rounds.

Life can be shocking,
you only have to look at the news to see.
I sometimes wonder does this trouble everyone?
Or is it only me?

Life can be tragic, with little hope and full of sorrow.
I sometimes think that this will all clear up and be better
tomorrow.

But...

I sometimes see little signs of hope, like a cheery hello!
Life can be fun and cheerful, if you go with the flow.
I sometimes see little miracles like a new-born baby's smile.
Life can be amazing if you stop and share a while.

I sometimes see video clips of people helping others.
Life can be great if you show compassion to one another.
I sometimes hear of people who have conquered adversity,
trouble and tests.
Life is awesome! Joyous!  Celebrate! Life is the best!

## 51    <u>Life has its ups and downs</u>

Life has its ups and downs.
Life has its highs and lows.
Life has mights and maybes.
Life has knows and I don't knows.


It's hard to be happy and positive,
when life has you between a rock and a hard place.
Life can be tricky and catch you out,
and it's hard to keep a smile on your face.


Look for the positives, life is great!
Unhappiness is like a prison.
I think I've found the secret to life,
and happiness...it's called optimism!

## 52    Live forever

If I'd known that I was going to live this long,
I'd have taken better care of myself.
I suppose I should be thankful that,
I still have my own teeth, hair and health.

I could have worked a bit harder,
at being lithe and trim and thinner.
But, it's the puddings that I blame,
because I hardly ever ate any dinner.

I believe we are all here for a reason.
We all have a destiny to pursue.
But at the moment I seem to be on the fast track,
because I feel that I'm pursuing quite a few!

Family, gardening, baking, handicrafts, ukulele,
Church, walking, reading and poetry.
Guess there's plenty that is keeping me going,
plenty to occupy and define me.

There's so much in life for me to achieve.
I've a plan on how to do it...and it's clever.
I've just got to keep on going and to fit it all in...
...well the only way...is for me to live forever!

## 53    Pooh sticks

I always enjoyed reading AA Milne,
and the stories of Winnie the Pooh.
And ever since I read about the game Pooh Sticks...
...well...it's something I've always wanted to do.

To be out in the country with a best friend...
....to be on a bridge throwing sticks into a flowing stream.
To see which stick would be the winner...
....well it's always been a childhood dream!

So, imagine my delight, now in my sixtieth year,
to get such a surprise in the post.
My very own Bowel Cancer screening kit!
Poo sticks! How lovely! How gross!

Well, I won't be throwing these off bridges,
but using them in the privacy of my loo!
It's good that the NHS want to test me,
but...really... with my poo?

Sorry for this subject matter today,
but you must know me quite a bit.
Because...nothing ever happens in my life,
without a poem being written about it.

So, if you're a certain age and you get this pack,
Use it! Don't throw it away or say nix!
Prevention is better than cure!
So, be sure to use those poo sticks!

## 54    Secret to life

I think that I've discovered the secret to life,
and it's taken me nearly sixty years!
Make the best of what life throws at you.
It's better to accept it with smiles rather than tears.

Accept everything that comes your way.
Acceptance is a universal truth.
Now...that I've got life all sussed out,
I'm going to search for the secret of eternal youth!

## 55    When life sends you a challenge

When life sends you a challenge,
run towards it and embrace it.
Don't be put off by ifs and buts.
Don't be afraid, just face it.

What's the worst that can happen?
You'll never know if you run the other way.
Challenges are to be overcome.
There are new ones every day!

Don't say that you can't do it.
How do you know until you try?
If you don't grab hold of opportunity,
then life will pass you by.

Make the most of what life sends you.
Each day you can start anew!
Accept those challenges. Be amazed!
You never know what you can do!

*On paper, I'm very brave. In real life – I'm proper mardy!*

## Men

56        Bedroom satisfaction

He lured me into his boudoir,
with the promise of a meaty surprise.
He said, "When you see the size of it,
you won't believe your eyes!"

He seduced me with promises of satisfaction.
He said he had a tasty treat.
I was weak with anticipation,
as he whisked me off my feet!

He assured me that I'd be pleasured.
He gave me a full guarantee.
He said that he'd completely fill me,
Oh my! Whatever can this be?

He told me he'd share his bedroom secrets,
I was in for a great surprise!
And...Then when I was all atremble,
he...served up chips and two pukka pies!

Now... I know we need to spice up our sex life.
Perhaps he could dress as a cowboy? Or a trucker?
But pie and chips in the love nest?
Honestly he is a cheeky pukka!

*This poem was inspired by a Pukka pie poster in a Bulwell
chip shop. It showed a couple in bed sharing a pie!*

## 57    My poem is too rude for the chip shop

I crafted a poem, a while ago,
about the delights of pie and chips in bed.
I emailed it to Pukka Pies,
"Very good! What a talent!" they said.


They sent me a really super thank you,
a great big package arrived in the post!
A baseball cap, two mugs, pens and six posters,
but not the poster, that I'd like the most.


I thought I'd take my poem to the chip shop,
I was excited and really quite animated.
I printed it off in a good font, added a bit of clipart,
I even went to the trouble to have it laminated.


I called into the chip shop today,
my poem was nowhere to be seen.
I asked the fish fryer (I know him),
"Where's my poem? What does this mean?"


Well...he glanced up towards the poster,
of the couple with those Pukka pies,
then he came and stood beside me...
...and what he said was a big surprise.

"Your poem is too rude for this chip shop,
although we thought it funny, great and swell.
We can't go putting innuendo on our walls,
we have to think of the sensitivities of our clientele".


I nodded and looked up at the poster,
of that couple in the bed with the pie.
"But what about this picture...almost porn?
my poem would look great nearby!"


"Your poem is too rude for this chip shop,
although we thought it funny, great and swell.
We can't go putting innuendo on our walls,
we have to think of the sensitivities of our clientele."


He told me that they had all sorts of customers,
he didn't want to cause a fuss or a strop,
and although they liked my poem...
....well it was just too rude for this chip shop!


*If you live in Bulwell – you'll know this chip shop near the market – best chips in Bulwell!*

I thought you were immortal.
I thought you'd never die.
But...when I saw the news...
...well it really made me cry.

I think you were the first man,
that gave me chills and palpitations.
One kiss (or bite) from you...
...sending me off to eternal damnations.

I'd lie in bed for hours...
....panicking that into my room you'd fly.
I knew I'd not be able to resist...
...the stare of your hypnotic eye.

I must have watched all of your films;
I never thought that you'd expire.
Christopher Lee, you were a great star...
...remembered as the world's best vampire!

Of course you have starred in other films.
Bond films, Star Wars, Lord of the Rings...to name a few,
you were often cast as a villain...
...Your staring eyes made us believe it was true!

So...Christopher Lee, Rest In Peace.
To me you were always spectacular.
You always made me shiver and quiver with fright...
....Christopher Lee, you were an amazing Dracula!

I'd like to be wined and dined...
...I'm not sure how you feel?
But...isn't it about time...
...that we went out and had a romantic meal?

You're always taking me to Wetherspoons,
and today I think you were having a laugh,
because after we'd been out walking,
well...we ended up in Morrison's caff!

It's nice to eat out and have a chat;
it's something we often do.
But...could we have a change...sometimes...
...Maybe try something romantic...and new?

A candlelit supper, with wine and roses?
What am I thinking? It's all to no avail!
I'm stuck with a male who prefers a bargain,
pie and chips and a glass of real ale!

*Dedicated to Denis Rice*

I visited Nottingham today...
 he would think?
amazed at all of the inns,
 here he could get a drink!

I wonder if he'd go to Ye Olde Trip to Jerusalem,
Nottingham's (and England's!) oldest pub.
And, if he was feeling peckish...
... there are so many places in town to get some tasty grub!

Maybe he'd go to the Castle Rock brewery,
to sample some local real ale and fine beers?
I can imagine him supping and chatting with the locals,
I bet he'd be buying a round! Cheers!

If Robin Hood visited Nottingham today...
I wonder what he would say?
When he sees our transport system.
So much more efficient than in his day!

He could buy a one day kangaroo ticket,
and hop all over the city, by bus.
And if he wanted to go to Beeston or Clifton,
then the tram could take him... without any fuss!

If Robin Hood visited Nottingham today...
If he came in the summer, would his face light up with glee?
For our Old Market Square is transformed by sand and stalls,
and suddenly there we have Nottingham on Sea!

Would he take his boots off and have a paddle?
I can just picture him having fun with Nottingham folk.

For Robin Hood was a man of the people,
he was just that kind of bloke.

If Robin Hood visited Nottingham today...
If he came in October he could go to Goose Fair.
I wonder if he'd go on the Waltzers?
Or the big wheel to see Nottingham from the air?

I bet he'd be gobsmacked by all the activity,
and wonder what had happened to the geese?
But, I bet he'd enjoy a local delicacy...
...you can't go to Goose Fair without having mushy peas!

If Robin Hood visited Nottingham today...
If he came in the winter that would be grand.
For then he'd see the city centre all lit up,
and turned into a magnificent winter wonderland.

If Robin Hood visited Nottingham today...
There is so much to see and do!
So many places to visit -
I've only suggested one or two!

If Robin Hood visited Nottingham today...
I hope he'd be impressed by what he'd find.
People who strive for the best for where we live.
People who are caring, sharing and kind!

I hope that Robin would be proud of our fair city.
I hope that he would wish us all the very best of luck!
I bet he'd have a great big smile upon his face,
I bet he'd say "Ay up mi duck!"

*Suggested by Councillor Jackie Morris – Lord Mayor of
Nottingham. Now Sheriff of Nottingham for the second time!*

## 61  Richard of York Gained Battles in Vain

Richard of York Gained Battles in Vain.
The clues in the mnemonic - the clues in the name.
He came to do battle. He marched to Leicester.
But there he died, his bones left to fester.

He took the throne from his nephews - not a great uncle.
Shakespeare has maligned him as a nasty carbuncle.
And then came another claimant - Henry Tudor.
Making claims to the throne - what could be ruder?

So, off to Leicester to fight for England's throne,
little thinking he'd be lying dead and alone.
Bones lying for centuries alone in the dark,
what once was Greyfriars became a car park.

I wonder what those bones thought as they lay in the dust...
Of the Lords who let him down and betrayed his trust.
What would those bones say, if only they could talk?
I think they'd say, "Sorry Leicester but I'm Richard of York!"

So, whatever you think of the past and life's mystery.
It's all gone before - part of England's history.
If they could get up and those bones they could walk.
I think they'd be off and go back to York.

Sorry Leicester –
I know you've invested time and a lot of money.
You might not like my rhyme or think I'm being funny.
But, isn't it time that we stopped treating Richard so shabby?
Because...really... I think kings should be interred in
Westminster Abbey.

*Written before it was decided where Richard III should be*
*interred.*

## 62   Robin Hood's bones found!

Have you heard the latest?
Have you seen the news today?
They've been excavating bones and arrowheads,
down on Maid Marion Way.

The experts have been consulted.
Research has been done.
All that the archaeologists will say,
is that carbon dating has begun.

They say it's from the 13th century.
They say now, wouldn't it be good,
if all these bones and arrowheads,
belonged to the outlaw Robin Hood?

There's a garment with a label on,
R and H is what can be seen!
Must belong to Robin then,
because it's made in Lincoln Green.

Wouldn't it be really wonderful,
when all the world has seen and heard?
Nottingham's one up on Leicester (with our Robin),
because they've only got Richard the third.

Now Robin Hood was a legend!
It's said that he was a real good bloke.
What a pity that this news is fabricated...
...only an April Fool's  Day joke!

*Reported in the Evening Post 2014.*
*This was an April Fool's Day joke.*

It's always sad when someone dies.
There's shock and unbelief.
And when it's someone famous,
there's an outpouring of grief.

So, it is with Robin Williams,
a funny man, who had been around for years.
But, now on his sudden passing,
there is such sadness and many tears.

Robin brought a lot of happiness.
He was such a clever, witty man.
Ad-libbing, playing many roles,
Genii, Mork, Patch and Peter Pan.

But, underneath the laughter,
Robin had his troubles too.
Just goes to show that a man like him,
can be just like me and you.

A person might have celebrity,
with all the trappings of wealth.
But what good is that if you have addictions?
And troubled mental health?

So, remember Robin with fondness,
love and happiness too.
Goodbye Robin, Rest in Peace.
God bless! Nanu nanu!

## 64    Scotsmen

I'm a woman on a mission,
in Scotland on a quest,
peeking under Scotsman's kilts,
looking for the best...

I have it on good authority,
our cousin, Mari, knows,
that true, brave Scotsmen,
don't wear no underclothes.

She told me that (at a recent wedding),
each Scotsman lifted up his kilt,
surprising all the other guests,
to see these men were so well-built.

So...Now I am off down to Edinburgh,
going to the Golden Mile.
Who know what I might find there?
Maybe...something to make me smile?

Seeking out some tatties and neeps...
...Really have I no shame or guilt?
But...maybe I'll find the Loch Ness monster,
lurking underneath a kilt?

I'm impressed by all these braw Scotsmen,
It's a bit chilly...there's no heat wave.
The rain pours down into their sporrans.
No wonder they sing about Scotland the brave!

*Thanks to Mari McKay!*

## 65   Snoring!

When you are sleeping next to me, I lay there and think,
that your gentle breathing matches mine, at last we are in sync!

As I fall asleep to your rhythms,
like waves softly lapping at the shore.
Nothing prepares me for the tsunami,
when you suddenly start to snore!

You claim that you are a light sleeper,
you say that you never ever snore!
Flippin' 'eck, mister, you're noisier
than a banging outhouse door!

I whisper to you, "shush be quiet",
and try to push you over onto your side,
but, usually you roll right back,
snoring with your mouth open wide.

The snoring reaches a crescendo. I'm really at my wits end.
I no longer want you as a bed partner.
I don't think I'm even your friend!

I wouldn't mind ...but you deny,
that you even ever snore.
One of these days you're going to get,
pushed out onto the floor!

And...then when you snore yourself awake,
snoring loudly with a massive jolt!
You blame me! Say I woke you up.
You say it's all my fault!

You never say you are sorry, never show any remorse.
I'm thinking that snoring should become...

                            ...grounds for a divorce!

## 66    <u>Switch your mobile on!</u>

I'm really feeling irritated.
I'm really very vexed!
You never have your mobile switched on,
whenever I phone or text.


You say that it's always with you.
But only switched on for an emergency.
Has it never occurred to you...?
That the emergency might be from me!


You say let's keep in touch....
Well...that's a bit of a con...
How can I contact you?
If your bloody mobile's never on!


*Sorry for the swearing...but???*

***SWITCH YOUR MOBILE ON!***

## 67    We've never had to consult a solicitor yet.

We've been happy for 38 years.
Truly blessed with hardly any upset.
And as my husband says...
We've never had to consult a solicitor yet.

We've raised a family together.
Three of them we have beget.
And as my husband says...
"We've never had to consult a solicitor yet".

We've managed our finances,
Never borrowed or got into debt.
And as my husband says...
"We've never had to consult a solicitor yet".

We've lived a happy life.
Don't think there's any regret.
And as my husband says...
"We've never had to consult a solicitor yet".

We're learning new things together.
Maybe we'll do a ukulele duet?
And as my husband says...
"We've never had to consult a solicitor yet".

We hardly ever quarrel.
Thank God for the television set!
And as my husband says...
"We've never had to consult a solicitor yet".

We've had our ups and downs.
It's best that we forget.
And as my husband says...
"We've never had to consult a solicitor yet".

Ok, I'll tell you I wanted a new kitchen,
and he wanted a kitchenette,
And as my husband says...
"We've never had to consult a solicitor yet".

He takes his time and does jobs slowly.
Me - I'm like a supersonic jet.
And as my husband says...
"We've never had to consult a solicitor yet".

It takes allsorts - opposites attract.
I guess we make a perfect set.
And as my husband says...
"We've never had to consult a solicitor yet"

I saw something on Facebook,
that's made me giggle all day.
I once said someone was handsome,
in a Yul Brynner kind of way.

I must admit that I'd forgotten it,
but, it's really made my day,
that someone remembers me...
...in a Yul Brynner kind of way.

I guess this must be my mission!
Compliments I can pay,
by saying that certain gentlemen are handsome,
in a Yul Brynner kind of way.

*Dedicated to all those handsome 'Yul Brynner' types out there – especially Craig Cameron.*

## Oddities

69 <u>Camera phone</u>

Whoever thought of putting a camera in a phone?
Well I think that this idea is just grand!
If ever I met the person whose idea it was,
well, I'd have to shake their hand!

It's really such a great idea,
its revolutionised how we can communicate.
Now you can post artistic pictures,
of whatever meal is on your plate!

70 <u>Freddie is a good boy.</u>

Freddie is a good boy.
His Grandma's pride and joy.
Every day they got out for walkies,
and then come back for treats and talkies.
Snuggled up to watch 'Create and Craft',
3 doggies and a Grandma - oh how daft!

Now, Freddie and his sisters, Lucy and Flossie,
had their hair cut the other day.
Groomed and sleek and trim and glossy!
What smart dogs' people would say!

Grandma got the doggies ready;
off they went for their daily trot!
But, hang on! Where is Freddie?
Two dogs... not three... who is forgot?

What?? Freddie, was out in front,
running off at such a great speed.
For, now that he'd had his haircut,
he no longer fitted his harness or his lead.

Freddie, was off and running!
The little blighter wouldn't stop,
not even to do a whoopsie!
Or a wee at the bus stop!

Lucy and Flossie wanted to sprinkle and tinkle,
but, with Grandma, they had to run,
chasing after that unstoppable Freddie,
who thought that it was all such fun!

Freddie ran and ran and ran;
he could have run for miles!
He kept turning and looking at Grandma,
giving her doggie laughs and smiles!

"Freddie! Freddie!" Grandma shouted.
"Please stop, you naughty boy!"
People stopped and stared and wondered,
what was this hoi polloi?

"Freddie! Freddie!" Grandma implored,
"Please, Freddie will you stop?"
Poor Grandma was needing oxygen,
and she was only fit to drop.

This doggie - human race went on for ages.
Honestly...it's not a lie!
Grandma and girly dogs worried for Freddie,
as there was lots of traffic whizzing by!

Eventually, Grandma caught him.
My! She was cross and feeling grotty!
She shouted at her baby boy,
and smacked his little botty!

Grandma looked him in the eye;
Freddie and Grandma were face to face.
"Freddie you could have been killed!
You really are a flippin disgrace."

"Freddie! You're a bad boy!
You are not my pride and joy!
You really are a naughty dog!
Why do you have to run off and annoy?"

Back home, Freddie slunk away.
No 'Create and Craft' for him!
It wasn't his fault the harness didn't fit.
He'd lost weight through having a trim!

Later that night, Grandma got the call,
Mum, couldn't do a thing with Freddie.
He was sulking in his special place,
refused his tea - he wasn't ready!

Now...Grandma loved her Freddie truly,
and it's really no surprise,
that Grandma had to reassure Freddie,
tell him she loved him and apologise.

She'd only given him a little tap;
she was worried he'd be run over and squished!
She never meant to hurt his feelings,
that was something she'd never wished.

"Freddie, you are a good dog,
you are Grandma's pride and joy.
I love you to the moon and back,
you are my best, good boy!"

"I love your little smiley face,
all soft and sweet and furry.
But, please don't run off fast again...
....or I'll have to call you Freddie...Mercury!"

Freddie's' running off caused Grandma lots of stress
and palpitations!
Thank goodness it was just one dog...
...and not 101 Dalmatians!


*With thanks to Grandma, Sandra Clay, for this true story.*

## 71    My cat, Missy

You wake me with your cold wet nose,
and your whiskers in my face.
I don't think you understand,
that you are invading my personal space.

I thought it was George Clooney,
waking me for a bit of morning delight.
You haven't even woke me with a cup of tea;
you know this just ain't right!

You cry and whimper in my ear,
demanding breakfast and you want it NOW!
You bounce around the bedroom,
waking me with your loud Meow!

## 72    That's where the sea comes in...

That's where the sea comes in...but where do I begin?
Of Great Britain which beach do I love the most,
from all of your 19.5K miles of coast?
Because, in Great Britain our great seaside we can boast!
That's where the sea comes in...

That's where the sea comes in...
at old-fashioned Sutton (on sea) of course!
Waves sweeping and cleaning the beach with such force.
Starfish, crabs and shells but nary a seahorse.
Seagulls squawking and squabbling themselves hoarse.
Sea breezes carrying the vanilla scent of the gorse.
Sutton on Sea, our favourite, of course we endorse!
That's where the sea comes in...

That's where the sea comes in...
Beach huts standing on guard like soldiers on parade.
Pensioners mashing tea, while sat in their shade.
Children proud of the sand structures that they've made.
Donkey rides on the sands with friendly donkeys that brayed.
That's where the sea comes in...

That's where the sea comes in...
Kites dancing and fluttering in a windy gust.
Punch and Judy having a domestic. How Mr Punch cussed!
Sun-worshippers 'chilling'; anointed with sun cream, they're not fussed!
Day trippers in hoards, to the beach they've been bussed.
We British have really got this whole seaside lark sussed.
Thank goodness, our coast is protected by our National Trust!
That's where the sea comes in...

*Inspired by Dr John Cooper Clarke's poem for the National Trust. My friend, Pete Gill, suggested that I try to write in a similar style. Thanks Pete!*

## 73    The war will be over by Christmas

The war will be over by Christmas.
Let's join up - it will be a lark!
But, it wasn't so funny four years on,
in trenches, cold, damp and dark.

It's a long way to Tipperary.
It's a long way to Ypres and The Somme.
It's quicker to get to heaven,
when hit by a bullet or bomb.

Four years we've been fighting,
I can't remember what it's all been for.
Friends have died at my side.
Why can't we stop this war?

We thought that it would be an adventure.
We thought it would be fun.
We thought we'd get to see the world.
We thought we'd defeat The Hun.

But in war there are no winners.
In war there's only pain.
So, why haven't we learnt our lesson?
Why have wars again and again?

And so throughout the ages,
War rears its ugly head.
It seems that war is just about,
making people dead.

Why can't people get along?
Why can't we be friends?
Why does there have to be conflict?
Will warcraft ever end?

*Written to commemorate the 1914 -18 conflict.*

## 74     Waterworks

I know that I've had some problems in the past.
But, at the moment I'm on a roll.
I think that it's all water under the bridge,
and I've got my waterworks under control.

The pelvic floor exercises are working.
I'm drinking decaffeinated coffee and tea.
And I clench my muscles and try not to think,
of babbling brooks when I need to wee!

So, why are Boots sending me literature,
about incontinence pads?
And coupons for money off, too!
And why are WaterAid sending me mail,
about World Toilet Day?
Honestly! What is a girl with bladder issues to do?

I suppose it's just one of life's ironies,
that this data arrived in the same post, today.
Well, it gave me a laugh and material for a poem,
and that's all that I've got to say!

I know that my bladder problem,
in the past has been quite chronic.
So, I laughed till the tears ran down my leg!
So, maybe it's not so ironic!


*It's true! I did receive vouchers from Boots and literature
from WaterAid in the same post.*

## 75    We're not on the same wavelength

I don't think we are on the same wavelength.
You say things that I cannot comprehend.
I used to try to look as if I understood,
but now I can't be bothered to pretend.

You express yourself with complex terminology;
you have a complicated point of view.
I'm not very good with all these big words;
really...I haven't got a clue?

I think you pontificate because you are full...
of your importance...I don't like it one little bit!
I wish you would use normal language,
I wish you weren't so full of xxxx

*Funnily enough this isn't about Denis – but someone else.*

## 76     You'll never be on my quiz team!

I know as we get older...
...that we get forgetful and muddled a bit.
But, sometimes the things that you say,
really do take the biscuit!

I wonder if you either stop to think,
before you put your brain into gear.
Or do you just say the first thing,
that pops into your head? Really you're not that clear?

You really make me laugh out loud.
Your muddles make me scream!
But, I'm sorry you'll never be my 'phone a friend',
you'll never be on my quiz team!

*But this poem is! Much as I love him...sorry Denis!*

## Religious stuff

### 77    God loves me

God loves me – as intimately as a lover,
as compassionately as a brother,
unconditionally as a mother,
above and beyond any other – God loves me!

### 78    Green church cups

There are many religious factions, many churches,
political parties, community groups and stuff.
And... I should know as if been around quite a few,
and I've seen pretty much enough!

I've met many different types of people,
with many differing points of view,
most people I've respected, liked and got on well with...
...except for the odd one or two.

But...I've started to notice a common thread,
a unifying link through life's down and ups!
Because everywhere I go, on my travels,
all these folk are using the same green church cups!

Now, what is it with these old fashioned cups and saucers,
in that weird green shade of eau de nil?
Years ago, did some manufacturer make them
indestructible?
Because community groups are using them still!

I guess when they were originally purchased,
they must have been quite dear?
They look like something pre-war, pre-coronation,
and  they are definitely pre-Ikea!

It makes me chuckle whenever I see them,
a cuppa, in one of them, perks you up!
I bet they'll go on forever those antique,
notorious green church cups!

*I've been performing my poems at WI groups and social
groups in church halls and they nearly all have those green
cups! I found out that they are called Beryl.*


## 79    If Heaven has a flavour it must be coffee

"If Heaven has a flavour it must be coffee",
 the sign outside the cafe read.
But, do I really want to be tasting coffee,
when I'm in Heaven and I'm...dead?

I suppose when I am dead,
my taste buds no longer need to be sated.
So, it doesn't matter if I overdose on double chocolate
macchiato,
instead of decaffeinated.

If Heaven has a flavour,
I wonder what I'll get?
Sweet or sour or savoury,
fruit or chocolate?

I'm rather fond of strawberries,
raspberries and kiwifruit too.
But if I have to choose just one flavour,
then - go on - chocolate will have to do!

## 80    Lord's Prayer banned

I read that England is no longer a Christian country...
...and that sort of made me sad.
But then I thought we're multicultural!
And that really made me feel very glad.

There's a multicultural, multi faith advert,
of the Lord's Prayer,
featuring the diverse faiths and ethnicities from our glorious land.
It was due to be shown in the cinema,
before the new Star Wars film...

                              ...but sadly it has been banned.

'The powers that be' think that this prayer will offend people,
 and I wonder can that really be true?
For Jedi Knights are the seventh most popular religion...
...claiming that the force is always with you.

So, although this advert has been banned,
and won't be displayed on the big cinema screen.
The constant sharing and reposting on social media,
means that this advert will constantly be seen!

A Lord's Prayer featuring the many faiths and faces of England,
surely that must be worth a view?
Whether you be Christian, Muslim, Atheist or Jedi...
...I sincerely wish - May the Force always be with you!

*If you've not seen this advert then Google – justpray.uk or
https://www.youtube.com/watch?v=vlUXh4mx4gl*


*And now my version of the Lord's Prayer – written in a
Nottingham (Bulwell) dialect.*


Ay up, our Dad, in Heaven,
yor dead good, mi duk.
Yor Kingdom com,
Yor will 'appen 'ere
As it is at yor ahse.
Gizzus ow snap and ow cobs.
An' forgiv us from prattin abaht,
as we forgiv them as is prattin abaht to us.
Stop us from being suck-eh,
and  doin' owt batch-eh.
For yorz is t' kingdom,
T'clout and t'glory,
Allus and allus.
Tara.
XXX


*See Matthew 6:  9-13 for the Bible version.*

## Palm Sunday Donkey

I often wonder about that little donkey,
in that village, with his mum, safely hidden,
a donkey and her colt...
...and neither of them had been ridden.

I wonder what that donkey thought,
when those strangers came that day?
"The Master needs a donkey",
and then they took them both away.

I wonder if that donkey was frightened,
with her little heart fastly beating.
I bet that the Master calmed her,
with a gentle touch and greeting.

I wonder what that donkey thought,
as she approached the city?
People shouting, waving palm branches,
what a welcoming committee!

I wonder if that donkey felt proud,
as she carried that heavenly load,
carefully stepping over cloaks,
and branches cast onto the road.

I wonder if that donkey realised,
the burden that she (and the Master) bore.
Hosanna was the cry that day,
Gloria to God for evermore!

I wonder if that donkey knew,
that "Hosanna" would change to "Crucify"?
That the Master she was carrying triumphantly,
would be condemned to die.

I wonder if that donkey was aware,
as through the palms she carefully tread,
that before the week was over,
that the Master would be dead?

I wonder when that donkey noticed,
when that cross upon her back was perfected.
I wonder if it was on that first Easter day,
when the Master was resurrected?


*A lot of wondering in this poem!*
*If you are wondering look here - Matthew 21:1-11*

I'm not sure that I'm a Holy person,
perfect? No I ain't?
I'm just trying my best to be a good person,
I'm working towards being a saint.

I've never performed a miracle.
But, good deeds I've done a few.
I'm working towards being a saint,
trying to live a life that's pure and true.

It's hard trying to keep on the straight and narrow,
when temptation is everywhere.
Us saints-in-training can find life tricky,
trying to combat life with goodness and prayer.

So, when it's All Saint's Day think of me,
I'm a fallible human being, just like you.
But, with prayer and patience and positivity,
you could be a saint, like me, too!

Some people say Christians are cracked!
Of that, there is no doubt...
...for, surely, you have to be cracked,
to let your light shine out!

So, let your light shine in the darkness!
Sparkle wherever you go.
Don't worry if people think you're cracked...
....what do those people know?

Shine with the love of Jesus!
Illuminate the community in which you live.
Remember that life is not about taking,
it's also about what you have to give.

*I remember Jim Maddison, a great preacher and teacher, telling me a true story about a miner preaching down the mine. The other miners called him cracked and his response was that he had to be cracked to let the light shine out.*

*God Bless!*

Imagine...you're at a wedding reception,
the party is in full swing,
you fancy a top-up of your drink,
but there's no more wine to bring.

I wonder... What would the guests do,
would they scream and shout?
When they discover that all of the booze,
 has suddenly run out.

Envisage...that Jesus is a guest there;
I wonder what would Jesus do?
Fill up the water pots,
and pray over them to create a special brew!

Envision...he'd had to be a miracle maker;
he'd surely have to be divine,
to be able to take plain old water,
 and transform it into delicious wine.

Fancy? Not just any old wine either,
but wine of the very best quality.
The best vintage saved for last,
a wonderful blend and given out for free!

Now imagine...wonder...envision...indulge me if you can.
While, I ponder on the miraculous wonders from that
miracle man.

Our bodies are made up of water;
I read that it is at least sixty percent!
If Jesus changed our water into wine,
I wonder how we would ferment?

I hope that we'd be full and overflowing,
that we'd be sparkling and full of bubbles.
I hope that we'd have plenty of fizz to spare,
and laugh away all of life's troubles.

Imagine...we'd all be fizzy, full of life,
full of fun and full of love.
If Jesus transformed our water into wine...
...well glory to God above!

What wonders we could accomplish?
Heaven only knows.
I pray that I am up to the transformation,
 and that God's love overflows!


*Read the full story – John 2 1-11.*

## 85 When God closes a door, somewhere He opens a window.

Sometimes we choose to close a door ourselves,
and that chapter of our life ends.
We leave behind our old routine,
say farewell to colleagues and to friends.

There is sadness in our leaving.
We wonder how can we bear to part?
But, be assured that there will always be,
fond memories within our heart.

And...so we close that door.
There's a bright future to look forward to,
and there will always be possibilities,
plenty to try that is new!

The door closes, and we go through,
God opens a window of opportunity.
New things to discover, new chances to take,
new ways to engage with the community.

So look through that window,
enjoy that great view.
Remember that wherever you go,
that God will be there with you!

*Written when Pauline Lynch (Head Teacher) retired from
Our Lady's School, Bulwell. Her gift to the School was a
beautiful stained glass window.*

# Ukulele

86      Cajon

It was 'end of term' at the ukulele club;
we were singing, strumming and having fun.
When Annie asked if I'd like to play her Cajon,
quickly I agreed and said "ok you're done".

Now a Cajon is a special box that you sit upon,
when you play it makes a drumming sound.
But, this Cajon was Annie-sized...
...so my feet never touched the ground.

I had to lean forward and give the front,
a tap, a pummel, a beat and a bang,
and pretty soon I got into the rhythm,
yes I really truly got the hang!

Now, being 'end of term' we were playing novelty songs,
and the one that I enjoyed the best,
was the song about Ernie the milkman,
who drove the fastest milk cart in the west.

I was really getting into the swing of this Cajon,
enjoying the vibrations from all this percussion.
I could feel the vibrations through my nether regions,
and I was sitting there without the aid of a cushion.

Sitting there pleased with myself,
enjoying exploring making this drumming sound.
But don't forget this Cajon box was too big for me;
my feet never touched the ground!

The novelty songs we were playing got sillier,
we were singing, strumming and feeling great!
I was especially getting into the swing of it!
I loved the way this Cajon did pulsate!

Our last song was that Victoria Wood classic,
where the woman wants beating on her bottom with the
Woman's Weekly.
A song with many, many verses, each getting faster,
and I drummed, patted and played it so uniquely!

So...imagine the scene - getting faster and faster.
The beats - oh they did reverberate!
Everyone strumming at fever pitch,
and me on a box that did vibrate!

I'll leave you to draw your own conclusions!
but...flippin' 'eck we played at a great pace.
Now...I know the secret of the Cajon!
And I know why Annie's always got a smile on her face!

*Thanks to Annie Molyneux for letting me experience
playing her Cajon!*

## 87      I went on a trip to Blackpool

I went on a trip to Blackpool,
to the George Formby Society convention.
I saw lots of interesting singers,
singing Formby songs...too many to mention!

They all played their very best,
and everyone got a turn.
And it was sort of....interesting,
about George Formby, I did learn.

There was so much innuendo,
and several saucy remarks!
For, lots of the songs alluded to,
the privatest of a man's parts.

There was a song about a little ukulele,
and keeping it always in your hand.
I thought it wasn't the size that matters,
or did I misunderstand?

Another song, with a thinly disguised reference,
was about a stick of Blackpool rock.
I suppose back in pre PC days,
you couldn't sing about a xxxx

(something to shock).

*Inspired by a trip to the George Formby convention –
thanks Howard Walters!*

I'm wishing you a Ukulele Christmas.
May your Christmas be a happy tuneful time.
I wish that your Christmas can be spent,
full of joy and merriment.
I'm wishing you a Ukulele Christmas...in rhyme.

I'm wishing you a Ukulele Christmas.
May you always be striking just the right chord.
Let your Uke bring much happiness,
may your Christmastime be blessed.
Playing the Ukulele brings its' own reward.

I'm wishing you a Ukulele Christmas.
I pray that you will always be in tune.
However you celebrate,
playing your uke - will be just great.
A Uke spreads a smile, no-one is immune!

I'm wishing you a Ukulele Christmas.
May you always be in tune without everyone.
When winter nights are dark and dreary.
Strumming your Uke will make you feel cheery.
You can't beat a Uke and a happy Christmas song!

I'm wishing you a Ukulele Christmas.
May your playing always be a great success.
Whatever your religion, faith or creed,
Ukulele fills a spiritual need.
Happy Ukulele Christmas and God Bless!

## 89    New ukulele

I've heard you can play a good tune on an old fiddle.
So, just think what you could accomplish with a new ukulele!
You can practice your strumming or fingerpicking techniques,
you can give it a good plucking...daily.

## 90    Pointy bits

I have a little problem,
not sure if I should say.
But I'm wondering how to hold my ukulele,
'Cause my chest gets in the way.

I've tried holding my uke up high
I've tried it low... but it's not okay.
'Cause I've got pointy bits on my chest,
and they get in the way.

I've tried with and without a strap.
I've tried it this and that away.
But, I've got pointy bits on my chest,
and they get in the way.

I've tried strumming it frontwards.
I've tried it backwards and sideways.
But, I've got pointy bits on my chest,
and they get in the way.

I've asked around my ukey friends.
I've googled and looked on YouTube.
I've just noticed that my uke has a curvy bit,
that fits nicely underneath my boob.

So let's all sing and strum and be happy.
Let's practice every day.
I'm not troubled by pointy bits on my chest
They're no longer in the way.

## 91    Rolling instead of Rocking

I was playing great at the ukulele group,
but then...something shocking.
Suddenly I was rolling when I should have been rocking.

My strumming was all over the place,
I really must confess,
I was strumming up instead of down,
it was a musical mess!

My down down, up up, down up strokes,
were really not in sync,
I hoped no-one would notice,
I dread to think what would they think?

I couldn't get my rhythm right,
instead of fingers, I'd got thumbs.
I seemed to have lost the plot,
 and was messing up my strums!

I'm ok when we play at a slowish pace,
not that great when we play quick.
I know that I should practice more.
I'm just a three chord trick!

The latest craze that is hitting the scene,
the fad of most of the 'mature' population,
is taking up a new interest, a new hobby,
and playing the ukulele is the current sensation!

Most orchestras and groups have a strict dress code;
wearing smart black and white is usually enough.
To stand out from the crowd...
                         ...we thought we'd be different,
so, our orchestra decided to perform in the buff.

There were all sorts of comments from the players,
and some of us had very real concerns.
Arthur didn't mind stripping off to his vest and pants,
but the thought of bare bosoms brought on one of his turns.

Sybil didn't mind showing off her personal piercings.
While George was embarrassed by his raunchy tattoos.
Martha cast her clouts off with gay abandon,
but insisted on keeping on her blue suede shoes.

Fred didn't mind showing off his piccolo,
he only ever got it out on special occasions.
He kept it cleaned and polished to show the ladies.
Now he was ready to exhibit it to the nations!

Harvey had a penchant for playing with bells and whistles,
playing them, whilst naked, had him vexed.
He worried that his kazoo playing sent out the wrong
message,
and the audience might think he was oversexed.

Some of the orchestra decided "if you've got it...
...better flaunt it"...
    ...and didn't even mind to beg your pardon.
Tummies tucked in, legs waxed and bodies baby oiled,
and our Mavis even went and trimmed her lady garden.

Suddenly, everyone switched to playing baritones,
so much bigger to cover up their private bits.
Some of the ladies purchased extra-large tuners,
conveniently placed to cover up their tits.

The orchestra was an overnight success story.
Our nakedness caused wonder, mirth and fun.
But, the highlight of the group was Naughty Annie,
the mistress of the unique and wondrous Cajon!

Our orchestra is such an inspiration,
nudity and the over fifties are just the job!
We sing and strum and are really very happy...
...and we've given new meaning to the expression –
                flash mob!


*All names changed to protect the innocent!*

It was a quiet Thursday evening,
we were in TV–watching-mode,
when we heard a pop, like a champagne cork.
Flippin eck did our ukulele just explode?

Calmly watching TV,
how could we ever anticipate or knowed...
...that minutes later ...POP!
Flippin eck did our ukulele just explode?

It was the first one that we had bought,
our love and care for it overflowed.
This lovely little soprano uke.
Flippin eck did our ukulele just explode?

We loved that little ukulele,
often playing it 'a la mode',
we treated it with kindness.
Flippin eck did our ukulele just explode?

It wasn't a cheap one either,
and it wasn't warped or bowed.
It was played many times daily.
That lovely little soprano ukulele.
Flippin eck did our ukulele just explode?

*This really happened!*
*A loud bang and a broken ukulele!*

## 94  Ukulele blues.

Now, I'm just a simple gal,
a simple life is what I choose,
but, since you've discovered the ukulele,
I've got those born again ukulele blues.

You've embraced all things ukulele,
like once you embraced me.
Now, our life us full of ukulele stuff,
no longer am I free.

You're a born again ukulele player,
full of passion for this thing.
You've always got it in your hands,
strumming and having a sing.

You're full of religious fervour,
for all things ukulele.
Concert, Soprano, Tenor, Baritone.
You're on the damn things, daily.

You're working on your plucking.
You no longer desire to pluck me.
What is it with that ukulele?
I wonder...what can it be?

I'm really easy to please.
Although I can't always enthuse.
But, since you've discovered the ukulele,
I've got those born again ukulele blues.

## 95     Ukulele-itis

Some people get addicted to all sorts,
drugs, beer, wine, chocolate and smack.
But, once you're hooked onto the ukulele...
...Well...I'm sorry...there's no turning back.

You start off with a little one,
you've heard that sopranos are the best,
But soon, you're hungry for more,
and ready to sample the rest.

You'll just try a little concert,
because, let's face it, everybody does.
And soon you're really into it,
enjoying that ukulele buzz!

Before you know it,
you need lots of extra things.
Bags to put the damn things in,
and extra sets of strings.

You try to fight this addiction.
You resist the temptation daily.
But, who are you really kidding,
you can't resist that ukulele.

Before long you're in and out of charity shops,
hoping for that rare bargain that you might discover.
Then progressing to wasting time on eBay,
hoping to buy...yet another.

You're working your way through the whole uke family,
I can hear you wail and moan,
I must just have this tenor uke,
then, next you'll be wanting a baritone!

There really ought to be somewhere,
where you can get help for this affliction.
Really, is there no help,
for someone suffering from ukulele addiction?

Someone ought to find a cure for this,
and they ought to make it snappy!
But... In the meanwhile there's an orchestra,
where you can sing and strum and be happy!


*Thanks to the Nottingham Ukulele Orchestra and the
Strictly Ukes (Mapperley Golf Club) for accepting us and
providing lots of inspiration for poems and songs!*

*www.nottinghamukeclub.com*

## Women

96      <u>A copper haired girl</u>

A copper-haired girl walked down our street,
and she reminded me of you.
She walked with a wiggle and giggle,
just like you used to do.

With her converse boots and her ripped knee jeans,
she skipped on down the street.
Tossing her copper curls and flashing her smile,
at everyone she happened to meet.

I thought that you had come back.
For a moment...my heart missed a beat.
But, second glances proved me wrong,
as she passed me on the street.

So... I thought of you...on the other side of the world,
and I prayed a silent ' keep-you-safe' prayer.
I smiled at this other girl and I wished her well,
this beautiful stranger with the same copper hair.


*You'll know who this is about!*

## 97    <u>All of my bras have gone tight</u>

I try to be careful what I eat,
often choosing low-fat or lite.
So, why is it - that I've recently noticed,
that all of my bras have gone tight?

It's not because I've had a boob job,
and I've never thought that I might.
But, something is expanding up there,
as all of my bras have gone tight!

Sometimes, in the morning when dressing,
putting my bra on turns into a fight.
I can't get my bazooms reined in properly,
now that all of my bras have gone tight.

They're all bulging and spilling over.
God knows I must look a sight!
Struggling to get them contained,
because all of my bras have gone tight.

This struggle could go on for ever,
I'm sure there must be others who share my plight...
....unless I'm the only one in England,
suffering because all of my bras have gone tight.

The only thing that is helpful,
truly a comfort, a joy and delight,
at the end of the day when that bra comes off.
Yes! That really is a good night!

*If you are a woman, you will know the blessed relief of
taking your bra off!*

Why is it that clothes in the sales,
are either size 22 or size 8?
There's never anything that fits me,
or even makes me look great.


The clothes that I do like are way too small,
or else they'd fit someone like Miranda Hart.
And some of the fabrics and patterns,
put me off before I even start!


What were the designers thinking?
I think some of them were have a laugh!
Because, let's face it, some of these dresses,
and designs are really terribly naff!


I've seen loads of crappy clothes today.
They go from bad to worse.
Just think of all the money that I've saved,
by leaving my debit card in my purse!

## 99  Dimples

I've just read that dimples are making a comeback!
Well, I never knew that dimples had fallen out of grace,
because, I've been walking around for x-amount of years,
with a lovely little dimple on my face.

It's a lovely little dimple on my chin!
All of my family have got 'em.
Dimples in our chins and in our cheeks,
and we've even dimples in our bottom!

*The dimples that are making a comeback are dimpled beer mugs.*


## 100  Everything I've got, today, is aching.

Everything I've got, today, is aching.
My head is throbbing fit to burst.
My boobs feel like two bricks on my chest.
I'm not sure where the aching is the worst.

My feet are flippin' killing me!
My calves are feeling tight!
My knees - well just don't go there...
I'm really not feeling at all quite right.

Everything I've got today is aching.
My eyes have gone all itchy and quite red.
I think I'll give this day a miss,
just have a duvet day and get back in my bed!

## 101    Goodbye

I'm waving you a good bye.
A bye that's full of hope.
I'm waving you a good bye,
knowing that you will cope.

I'm blowing kisses to you.
Each kiss full of love and care.
I'm blowing kisses to you,
each kiss a little prayer.

I'm giving you a big hug,
to send you on your way.
I'm waiting with another hug,
to give when you return another day.

I'm sending you off with positive thoughts.
I'm wishing you all the best.
I'm proud of you, son, you know that.
I know you'll pass any trial or test.

I'm waving, kissing, hugging.
I'm wishing you a good Goodbye.
I'm being brave and carefree.
I won't let you see me cry.

It's worse than when you started school,
then I could stand at the school gates and cry.
So, I'm waiting till you're on your way,
before I have a little cry.

*Suggested by and written for Pauline Whately.*

I can tell you tales of my old Mam...
...but, where should I begin?
The most treasured thing that she bequeathed to me,
was her old wooden rolling pin.

Now, if rolling pins could talk...
...this one a tale I'm sure it could spin.
It's seen some life and rolled out plenty of pastry ...
...me Mam's old wooden rolling pin.

When I was a rebellious teenager,
tempted by all kinds of vice and sin.
What kept me on the straight and narrow was a
smack from,
...me Mam's old wooden rolling pin.

Me Dad never stopped at the pub too late,
he knew what time he had to get in.
And he'd better come home sober or else...
...he'd face me Mam's old wooden rolling pin.

Me Mam's old rolling pin is magic!
Pastries disappear into air that's thin!
As fast as I can make and bake 'em ,
with me Mam's old wooden rolling pin.

Me Mam's pin is an original,
quite unique, without a twin.
There's only one and I've got it!
Me Mam's old wooden rolling pin.

One day when I am dead and gone.
I shall bequeath it to one of my kin.
My grandson's next in line for...
...me Mam's old wooden rolling pin.

And when I broke the news to him,
you should have seen him grin.
He can't wait for me to pop my clogs...
...so he can get his hands on...
...me Mam's old wooden rolling pin

*So here it is on record that Oliver inherits the rolling pin!*

103    Menopause!

When writing about the menopause,
where should I begin?
Should I tell you about the weight gain,
or the extra whiskers on my chin?

Should I tell you about the hot flushes,
that make you sweat and sweat?
Or maybe you'll be lucky and this isn't one,
of the symptoms that you'll get?

Better tell you to keep your fluids up,
you know that drinking water makes good sense.
It helps to keep you hydrated,
and stops you from feeling tense.

You might experience strange symptoms,
after all it is called 'The Change',
You might get broody and nesting,
and the furniture re-arrange.

You might feel that this is your last chance,
 and think about having another baby.
Girl, are you for real?
It's your hormones saying – yes or no or maybe!

Your emotions might be all over the place,
sometimes happy, sometimes sad.
Forget the trials of PMS,
because the menopause can make you mad!

Everything will start to dry up....your hair...
..your skin and your lady bits....
You might find that you've put on weight,
 and that none of your clothes fits.


But - look this is only another stage in life,
something that you will get through.
I find that it helps to not brood on it,
 and have a positive point of view.

There's lots of advice and help out there,
you'll get this menopause beaten yet!
See your Doctor, ask a friend or look on the internet.

Embrace the menopause,
is my advice – and I'll tell you what...
...Take good care of your body!
It's the only one that you've got.


*I was asked if I had a poem about the menopause.*
*I hadn't! So, I wrote this for Jasmin Vassell.*

## 104    Mother knows best

Have you brushed your hair today?
Have you cleaned your teeth?
Have you got clean knickers on?
It's important to be pristine underneath!

You might be in an accident!
You might be knocked over by a bus!
And if you haven't got clean knickers on...
...well goodness... There might be a fuss!

If a bus was to knock me over...
Then I don't think I'd have much of a chance.
And the last thing that I'd be bothered about,
is if I was wearing clean pants!


## 105  Mothers are founts of all knowledge.

Mothers are founts of all knowledge.
They have advice and sayings that are wise.
Such as...don't sit too close to the telly,
or else you will get square eyes.

And whilst we are on the subject,
if you want to be a bright spark,
remember to eat up all of your veggies,
as carrots help you to see in the dark!

You had to do stuff "because she said so",
or else you had to wait till your father got in.
And whatever you did, it was never quite right;
with mothers you never can win.

You had to keep your bedroom tidy,
and never leave toys or clothes on the floor,
and unless "you were born in a barn",
make sure you always closed the door!

Dinners had to be all eaten,
or else no pudding would you get.
It was no use trying to fool your mum,
because, Mothers never forget!

Eat up all your crusts of bread,
or you will never have curly hair.
Remember to close your mouth while you are eating.
And, for goodness sake, never swing on your chair!

Sometimes mothers asked stupid questions,
"What did you last slave die of?" is a favourite one.
And answering back isn't the correct response,
because cheekiness is frowned upon.

She's told you a thousand times,
that you really shouldn't exaggerate,
and she'll tell you another thousand,
that you'll be the death of her and get her in a state!

If ever you dared to make a funny face,
the wind might change...and oh my dears...
You'd stay with a funny face for ever;
as mother said, "it will all end in tears!"

My mum was always plumping up cushions,
and cleaning like a woman demented.
I think she must have had OCD,
before it was fashionable...or even invented!

A feather duster in her hand,
Mum was always on fine fettle,
and woe betide any smuts or dust,
if they ever tried to settle.

Carpets hanging on the washing line,
Mum whacking them with a beater or a broom.
I can still remember her happiness,
when our Dad bought her a vacuum.

Then vacuuming all the rooms,
it had to be done every day.
Everything spick and span,
or 'bottoming it' as Mum would say.

Washing clothes on Monday. Ironing on Tuesday!
Finding cleaning tasks to do, on every single day.

Beds made as soon as you were up,
nothing to be out of place.
Everything tidied away.
No clutter, not a trace!

Baking on Friday for the weekend,
with flour dust everywhere.
I don't know how she did it;
it must have driven her spare!

So, thinking back, I guess that...
...she must have had undiagnosed OCD,
I really must stop plumping up cushions,
as I think it's happening to me!

<u>Tea at Grandma's</u>

Every Sunday afternoon, I remember,
we had tea at Grandma's house,
and I had to sit there in my Sunday best,
as quiet as a mouse.

It was in the early sixties,
and really it's absurd,
that Grandma still believed that children
should be seen and never heard!

We all had to put on our bestest clothes,
and we all had to behave.
And Dad would grumble because Mum,
would insist he dress up and make him have a shave.

When it was to time for us to eat,
Grandma fed us salmon from the tiniest little tin,
lettuce, beetroot and lots of bread,
but she'd have to say Grace before we could tuck in.

Afterwards there would be tinned fruit,
served with a nice bit of tinned evap,
plus more bread and butter,
and we had to eat up every last scrap!

I'd have sit all prim and proper,
because that's what a good girl should do,
and I couldn't gobble down my tea,
I've have to daintily nibble and chew.

The adults would sit chatting,
boring stuff, talking on and on for hours,
if they had things to say that I wasn't to hear,
they'd send me into the garden to look at the flowers.

There was nothing much for me to do,
so, if I was really lucky,
they'd let me go outside to play,
but, only if I promised not to get mucky.

Time to leave; I'd have to kiss all the aunties,
with their whiskers and their smell of lavender water.
I'd have to mind my manners,
smile and be a polite granddaughter.

I never enjoyed Grandma's teas that much.
My opinion they never did seek.
If ever I was asked if I was visiting again.
I'd meekly say, "See you again next week!"


*Remembering Grandma Shellam, Aunties Pem, Nell
and Mabel.*

They rough and tumble into the house.
Trouble! Looking for fun and games!
Two boisterous grandchildren,
Havoc and Turmoil are their names.

There's no set times for their visits.
They can come whenever they please.
There's always tea and biscuits,
and a hug while sat on Grandma's knees.

There's always plenty to play with,
cars, books and toys galore.
And if they want to do some crafting,
Grandma's got a secret handicraft store.

If they want to play in the garden,
they can run around and scream and shout.
There's veg and flowers for the picking,
and a football to kick about.

There's food that's fun to eat.
At this Grandma's there are no high teas,
sausage cobs or pizzas, easy stuff to eat,
whilst watching favourite DVDs.

The time passes by too quickly,
and leaving time comes around too soon.
But, Havoc and Turmoil know that,
they are always welcome for another fun afternoon!

*For my lovely grandchildren – Abbigail and Oliver.*
*I love you both!*

There's a well-known organisation...
... that I've heard likes to makes jams and chutneys out of fruit.
Yes! I think that you've guessed it!
I'm referring to the Women's Institute!

They are welcoming to all types of women,
the good, the bad, the ugly and the cute!
Yes! You'll be met with open arms...
... at the Women's Institute.

They enjoy a laugh and a giggle. These gals are really a hoot!
So if you want to have a good night out,
come to the Women's Institute!

There once was a bit of an uproar...
...when they posed for that calendar...
... just wearing their birthday suit.
It was all for a good cause raising money for cancer treatment,
those barefaced ladies of the Women's institute!

I've heard that they want to spread the word.
Maybe you'll be a new recruit?
They are open to all ages, sizes and types of women,
at the Women's institute!

So, if you want to make new friends,
try a new hobby or a new craft pursuit.
Then join this bunch of skilled ladies,
at your local Women's Institute!

The WI has just celebrated their centenary!
I think that deserves a ten gun salute!
Congratulations and best wishes, ladies, lasses and gals
of the Women's Institute!

*Written in response to a request by my good friend,*
*Mollie Smith, and shared with several WI groups.*

I've been thinking about my Mum just lately,
and I really don't know why.
Sometimes I think of her and chuckle,
other times I just want to cry.

Now, my Mum would want me to be happy,
she always strove for the very best for me.
She guided me and was a great example,
encouraging me to be the best that I can be!

Mum taught me good old plain cooking,
sharing her knowledge and wisdom with me.
She showed me how to make a little go a long way,
taught me thrift and how to adapt a recipe.

She encouraged me to get a good education,
to always search and satisfy that learning need.
She taught me how to share what I have with others,
and not to be consumed by envy or greed.

Mum had a great sense of humour.
I hope I've inherited her sense of fun.
Finding fun in everyday situations,
laughing so hard that tears began to run.

Now, Mum wasn't a saint just an ordinary person,
with foibles and quirks the same as you and me.
She drove me crazy with her constant tidying,
and I think that she's passed on her OCD!

I only had my Mum for a short while,
but her influence is there for all to see.
For her love, care, example and guidance...
...has shaped the person that is me.

You are living the life that I should have been living.
You are doing the things that I should have done.
You are off experiencing life and having adventures.
You are out there having lots of fun!

It's not that I'm jealous of you;
I'm fairly content with my lot.
I'm happy with my own life.
But...sometimes I'm envious of what you have got.

You are living life to the limits,
and you are bravely doing it on your own.
I don't know if I could 'seize the day' like you have,
I'm content in my own comfort zone.

So, I can take pleasure in observing your life,
looking at photos of places where you have been.
Looking at life through your eyes,
seeing the great things that you have seen.

I'll never experience what you are doing.
I doubt that I'll ever do half of what you do.
Enjoy your life and share it with me,
so, that I can share a little bit with you!


*Inspired by my daughter, Heather (the copper haired girl!
Poem 96).*

Thank you for buying this book. If it was bought for you as a gift – then thank your friend! Hopefully, you will dip into this book from time to time and find a poem to make you laugh, cry, ponder, wonder and think...but mostly to make you laugh!

If you like my poems check out my Facebook page –
**Joy's Poems.**
Website- www.joyrice.co.uk
or email me on joyricepoet@gmail.com

I am available (for a fee) to entertain your social group with poems, anecdotes and songs.

And as this book is called Second Helpings (of Ecstatic Pudding) here's my Dad's Sugar Butty recipe written in Nottingham dialect.

T' mek a sugar butty

Fost oppen packet o Wonderloaf an gerra slice o bread.
Nex grab some butta or sum o that fancy marge spread.
Larup bread wi marge an cover all t' slice,
sprinkle on sum sugar to mek bread taste rate nice.

Fold bread in 'alf and tek a grett big bite.
If it's sweet an crunchy then yo've med a sugar butty orlrite!

This is me Dad's recipe for mekkin a sugar butty.
So nah yo've gorrit, don't get lairy, mardy or nutty.
An if yo' play ya cards rite, an cum to mi haus soon,
I'll show you how to mek a condensed milk sandwich,
 an if you're good I'll let ya lick the spoon!

*Enjoy!*